MW00947733

DESTINATION IRELAND: A TRAVEL GUIDE

Georgina Rollins

1

Copyright ©2024 by [Georgina Rollins]

All rights reserved. No part of this publication may be reproduced, distributed, or transmitted in any form or by any means, including photocopying, recording, or other electronic or mechanical methods, without the prior written permission of the publisher, except in the case of brief quotations embodied in critical reviews and certain other noncommercial uses permitted by copyright law.

Table of Contents

3

4

Introduction

Welcome to Ireland, a land of ancient legends, stunning landscapes, and warm hospitality. Nestled in the northwestern corner of Europe, Ireland captivates visitors with its rich history, vibrant culture, and breathtaking natural beauty. From the vibrant streets of its cities to the rugged cliffs along its coastlines, Ireland offers a tapestry of experiences that appeal to travelers of all ages and interests.

History

Ireland's history is a tapestry woven with tales of ancient Celts, Viking invaders, medieval kings, and centuries of struggle for independence. From the prehistoric monuments of Newgrange and Tara to the medieval castles dotting the countryside, Ireland's past is palpable at every turn. Visitors can explore the ruins of monastic settlements, walk in the footsteps of literary giants like James Joyce and

W.B. Yeats, and delve into the turbulent history of the Irish diaspora.

Culture

Ireland's culture is as rich and varied as its history. Music and dance are at the heart of Irish life, with traditional sessions taking place in pubs and cultural centers across the country. The literary tradition runs deep, with Ireland boasting a long list of esteemed writers, poets, and playwrights. Visitors can immerse themselves in the vibrant arts scene, attend a traditional Irish storytelling session, or explore the country's rich folklore and mythology.

Landscapes

From the windswept cliffs of the Wild Atlantic Way to the serene beauty of the Irish Midlands, Ireland's landscapes are nothing short of spectacular. The country's rugged coastline is dotted with picturesque fishing villages, sandy beaches, and dramatic sea stacks, while its lush interior is home to rolling green hills, tranquil lakes, and ancient forests. Outdoor enthusiasts will find endless opportunities for hiking, cycling, fishing, and golfing amidst some of the most breathtaking scenery in Europe.

Hospitality

Ireland is renowned for its warm hospitality and friendly locals. Visitors will find a warm welcome wherever they go, whether it's in a cozy pub, a charming bed and breakfast, or a bustling city street. The Irish are known for their love of conversation and craic (good times), and travelers are sure to make new friends and create lasting memories during their time in the Emerald Isle.

Ireland is a country that captivates the imagination and touches the soul. Whether you're exploring its ancient landmarks, immersing yourself in its vibrant culture, or simply soaking in its stunning scenery, Ireland offers a travel experience like no other. So pack your bags, prepare to be enchanted, and get ready for the journey of a lifetime in the land of saints and scholars, poets and rebels – welcome to Ireland.

About This Guide

Nestled in the northwestern corner of Europe, Ireland captivates visitors with its rich history, vibrant culture, and breathtaking natural beauty. From the vibrant streets of its cities to the rugged cliffs along its coastlines, Ireland offers a tapestry of experiences that appeal to travelers of all ages and interests.

History

Ireland's history is a tapestry woven with tales of ancient Celts, Viking invaders, medieval kings, and centuries of struggle for independence. From the prehistoric monuments of Newgrange and Tara to the medieval castles dotting the countryside, Ireland's past is palpable at every turn. Visitors can explore the ruins of monastic settlements, walk in the footsteps of literary giants like James Joyce and W.B. Yeats, and delve into the turbulent history of the Irish diaspora.

Culture

Ireland's culture is as rich and varied as its history. Music and dance are at the heart of Irish life, with traditional sessions taking place in pubs and cultural centers across the country. The literary tradition runs deep, with Ireland boasting a long list of esteemed writers, poets, and playwrights. Visitors can immerse themselves in the vibrant arts scene, attend a traditional Irish storytelling session, or explore the country's rich folklore and mythology.

Landscapes

From the windswept cliffs of the Wild Atlantic Way to the serene beauty of the Irish Midlands, Ireland's landscapes are nothing short of spectacular. The country's rugged coastline is dotted with picturesque fishing villages, sandy beaches, and dramatic sea stacks, while its lush interior is home to rolling green hills, tranquil lakes, and ancient forests. Outdoor enthusiasts will find endless opportunities for hiking, cycling, fishing, and golfing amidst some of the most breathtaking scenery in Europe.

Hospitality

Ireland is renowned for its warm hospitality and friendly locals. Visitors will find a warm welcome wherever they go, whether it's in a cozy pub, a charming bed and breakfast, or a bustling city street. The Irish are known for their love of conversation and craic (good times), and travelers are sure to make new friends and create lasting memories during their time in the Emerald Isle.

Ireland is a country that captivates the imagination and touches the soul. Whether you're exploring its ancient landmarks, immersing yourself in its vibrant culture, or simply soaking in its stunning scenery, Ireland offers a travel experience like no other. So pack your bags, prepare to be enchanted, and get ready for the journey of a lifetime in the land of saints and scholars, poets and rebels – welcome to Ireland.

Chapter 1. Getting Started

Planning Your Trip

Embarking on a journey to Ireland involves careful planning to ensure an enriching and memorable experience. Here's a comprehensive guide to help you navigate the process:

Research and Itinerary Planning

Begin by immersing yourself in research to uncover Ireland's top attractions, regions, and activities that align with your interests. Consider factors like weather, the time of year, and the duration of your stay as you craft your itinerary. Decide whether you want to focus on specific regions, such as Dublin, the Wild Atlantic Way, or the Ring of Kerry, or opt for a more extensive exploration of the entire country.

Transportation

Choose your mode of transportation based on your preferences and comfort level. Options include renting a car, utilizing public transportation, or joining guided tours. If driving, acquaint yourself with Ireland's road rules and driving conditions, including driving on the left side of the road. Explore public transportation alternatives like trains and buses for intercity and interregional travel.

Accommodation

Secure accommodations in advance, particularly during peak tourist seasons, to ensure availability and preferred locations. Consider a diverse range of options, such as hotels, bed and breakfasts, guesthouses, and self-catering accommodations, to experience different facets of Irish hospitality. Explore lodging choices in both urban and rural settings to fully immerse yourself in the Irish way of life.

Activities and Attractions

Compile a list of must-see attractions and experiences based on your interests, whether it's visiting historical landmarks, exploring natural wonders, or indulging in traditional music and culture. Consider booking tours or experiences in advance for popular attractions to secure your spot and optimize your time. Allow flexibility in your itinerary for spontaneous discoveries and unexpected adventures along the way.

Budgeting

Establish a realistic budget encompassing transportation, accommodation, dining, activities, and miscellaneous expenses. Research the cost of living in Ireland and factor in additional expenditures such as tipping and entrance fees. Look for opportunities to save money, such as opting for accommodations with complimentary breakfast or purchasing multi-attraction passes for discounted admission.

Packing

Pack appropriately for Ireland's varied weather conditions, including layers, waterproof outerwear, and comfortable walking shoes. Don't forget essentials like travel adapters, sunscreen, insect repellent, and any necessary medications. Consider bringing a daypack for excursions, along with a reusable water bottle and snacks for on-the-go sustenance.

Safety and Health

Stay informed about travel advisories and safety guidelines for Ireland before departure. Ensure you have comprehensive travel insurance covering medical emergencies, trip cancellations, and unforeseen circumstances. Familiarize yourself with emergency contacts and healthcare facilities in Ireland, especially if you have specific medical needs or conditions.

Cultural Etiquette

Respect and embrace Irish customs, greetings, and social norms to foster positive interactions with locals. Embody the spirit of Irish hospitality and engage in friendly conversations with residents. Honor cultural sites and traditions, adhering to guidelines and rules when visiting sacred or historical locations.

Entry Requirements and Visa Information

Entry into Ireland varies depending on your nationality and the purpose of your visit. Here's what you need to know:

Visa Requirements

Citizens of the European Union (EU), European Economic Area (EEA), and Switzerland can enter Ireland freely with a valid passport or national ID card. However, citizens of some EU/EEA countries may require an employment permit if planning to work in Ireland.

Citizens of certain countries, including the United States, Canada, Australia, and New Zealand, can visit Ireland for tourism or business purposes without a visa for stays of up to 90 days. However, they must have a valid passport and may need to provide additional documentation, such as proof of sufficient funds and a return ticket.

Nationals of other countries may require a visa to enter Ireland, depending on their nationality and the purpose of their visit. Visa requirements can vary, so it's essential to check with the Irish Naturalisation and Immigration Service (INIS) or the nearest Irish embassy or consulate for specific requirements.

There are two main types of visas for Ireland. The Short-Stay Visa, also known as the C Visa, permits stays of up to 90 days for tourism, business, or visiting family and friends. The Long-Stay Visa, or D Visa, is necessary for stays exceeding 90 days, such as for study, work, or family reunification.

The application process for visas typically involves submitting an application form, supporting documents (such as passport, proof of funds, and itinerary), and paying a fee. It's essential to apply well in advance of your planned travel dates to allow for processing time.

Immigration Control

Upon arrival in Ireland, travelers must go through immigration control, where their passports or travel documents will be checked. Non-EU/EEA/Swiss citizens may be required to provide additional documentation, such as proof of accommodation, return ticket, and sufficient funds for their stay. Immigration officers have the authority to grant or deny entry into Ireland based on various factors, including compliance with visa requirements and the purpose of the visit.

Visa Waiver Program

Ireland participates in the Visa Waiver Program (VWP) with the United States, allowing eligible travelers to enter Ireland for tourism or business purposes without a visa for stays of up to 90 days. Travelers entering under the VWP must register online through the Electronic System for Travel Authorization (ESTA) before traveling to Ireland.

It's essential to thoroughly research and understand the entry requirements and visa information specific to your nationality and the purpose of your visit to Ireland to ensure a smooth and hassle-free travel experience.

Best Time to Visit

Determining the best time to visit Ireland depends on various factors, including weather preferences, seasonal activities, and crowd levels. Here's a comprehensive guide to help you choose the ideal time for your Irish adventure.

Spring (March to May)
Spring is a delightful time to visit Ireland, with mild temperatures, blooming flowers, and longer daylight hours. The countryside bursts into life with vibrant green landscapes and colorful gardens. It's an excellent season for outdoor activities such as hiking, cycling, and exploring historic sites without the crowds that peak during the summer months. However, weather can be unpredictable, so it's advisable to pack layers and be prepared for occasional rain showers.

Summer (June to August)
Summer is the peak tourist season in Ireland, thanks to long daylight hours, warmer temperatures, and a full calendar of festivals and events. The countryside is lush and green, making it perfect for scenic drives along coastal routes like the Wild Atlantic Way or exploring picturesque villages in the countryside. Outdoor activities such as hiking, kayaking, and surfing are popular during

this time. However, expect larger crowds at popular attractions and higher prices for accommodations and activities. It's essential to book accommodations and tours well in advance, especially if traveling during the peak summer months.

Autumn (September to November)
Autumn in Ireland is a magical time marked by golden landscapes, crisp air, and fewer tourists compared to the summer months. The countryside transforms into a tapestry of red, orange, and yellow hues, making it ideal for scenic drives, leisurely walks, and photography enthusiasts. It's also harvest season, with farmers markets showcasing the best of Irish produce. While temperatures begin to cool, autumn is still relatively mild, and outdoor activities are enjoyable. It's a great time to experience the tranquility of rural Ireland and explore historic sites without the crowds.

Winter (December to February)
Winter in Ireland is characterized by shorter daylight hours, cooler temperatures, and occasional rain showers. While it's the quietest time for tourism, it's also a magical season to experience

Ireland's festive atmosphere and cozy charm. Cities like Dublin and Galway come alive with Christmas markets, festive lights, and traditional music sessions. Coastal towns offer opportunities for storm watching, while inland areas provide cozy retreats by the fireplace. It's an excellent time to immerse yourself in Irish culture through music, literature, and storytelling. While some attractions may have reduced hours or closures during the winter months, it's still possible to explore the country's historic sites, museums, and indoor attractions.

Ultimately, the best time to visit Ireland depends on your preferences, whether you prefer mild weather, vibrant festivals, or quieter moments to explore the countryside. Each season offers its own unique charm and experiences, ensuring that Ireland is a destination worth visiting year-round.

Packing Tips

Packing for a trip to Ireland requires careful consideration of the country's variable weather, outdoor activities, and cultural experiences. Here are comprehensive packing tips to help you prepare for your Irish adventure:

Clothing
Ireland's weather can be unpredictable, so bring clothing that can be easily layered to accommodate changing conditions. Include items like sweaters, lightweight jackets, waterproof outerwear, and scarves.

Comfortable shoes
Whether you're exploring cities, hiking along coastal trails, or wandering through historic sites, comfortable walking shoes are essential. Opt for sturdy footwear with good traction to navigate uneven terrain.

Rain gear
 Be prepared for rain showers by packing a waterproof jacket or coat, as well as an umbrella or rain poncho. Waterproof footwear, such as hiking boots or waterproof shoes, will also come in handy.

Warm accessories
Even in the summer months, evenings in Ireland can be cool, so pack items like hats, gloves, and warm socks to stay comfortable outdoors.

Casual and smart-casual attire
Ireland has a relaxed dress code, but you may want to bring a few nicer outfits for evenings out or special occasions. Casual clothing like jeans, t-shirts, and sweaters are suitable for everyday wear.

Tech and Accessories
Travel adapter
Ireland uses Type G electrical outlets, so be sure to pack a suitable travel adapter for charging your devices.

Camera
Capture the stunning landscapes, historic sites, and memorable moments of your trip with a camera or smartphone equipped with a good camera.

Reusable water bottle
Stay hydrated during your adventures by bringing a reusable water bottle. Tap water in Ireland is safe to

drink, so you can refill your bottle at accommodations or public drinking fountains.

Daypack
Carry essentials like water, snacks, a map, and a rain jacket in a lightweight daypack for day trips and sightseeing excursions.
Personal Essentials

Medications
Bring an ample supply of any prescription medications you may need, as well as over-the-counter remedies for common ailments like headaches, allergies, and upset stomachs.

Sunscreen
Even on overcast days, UV rays can penetrate clouds, so protect your skin by packing sunscreen with a high SPF rating.

Insect repellent
 If you plan to spend time outdoors, especially in rural areas or near water, consider bringing insect repellent to ward off mosquitoes and other biting insects.

Toiletries
Pack travel-sized toiletries like shampoo,
conditioner, soap, and toothpaste, as well as any
personal hygiene products you prefer.

Travel Documents

Passport
 Ensure your passport is valid for at least six
months beyond your planned departure date from
Ireland.

Travel insurance
Consider purchasing travel insurance to cover
unexpected medical emergencies, trip cancellations,
and other unforeseen events.

Tickets and reservations
Print or save electronic copies of your flight tickets,
accommodation reservations, and any tour or
activity bookings.

Itinerary and maps
 Have a printed or digital copy of your itinerary,
including addresses, contact information, and maps
for your destinations.

Miscellaneous
Reusable shopping bag
Ireland has implemented a plastic bag levy, so bring
a reusable shopping bag for carrying groceries,
souvenirs, or other purchases.

Currency
While credit and debit cards are widely accepted in
Ireland, it's a good idea to carry some cash for small
purchases, tipping, and emergencies.

Travel guidebook or apps
Enhance your travel experience with a guidebook or
travel apps that provide insights into Ireland's
attractions, dining options, and local customs.
By following these comprehensive packing tips,
you'll be well-prepared to enjoy your trip to Ireland
and make the most of its stunning landscapes,
historic sites, and cultural experiences.

26

Chapter 2. Understanding Ireland

Geography and Climate

Situated in the North Atlantic Ocean, Ireland is the third-largest island in Europe, covering an area of approximately 84,421 square kilometers (32,595 square miles). It is divided into two political entities: the Republic of Ireland, which occupies about five-sixths of the island, and Northern Ireland, which is part of the United Kingdom.

The landscape of Ireland is characterized by rolling green hills, rugged coastlines, and fertile plains. The central lowlands are flanked by mountain ranges such as the Wicklow Mountains and the MacGillycuddy's Reeks. The coastline is indented with numerous bays, peninsulas, and islands, including the iconic Cliffs of Moher and the Aran Islands.

Ireland's rivers, including the Shannon, the longest river in the British Isles, and the River Boyne, are vital features of the landscape, providing water for agriculture and hydroelectric power generation. The country's rich soil and temperate climate support agriculture, with Ireland known for its lush pastures, dairy farming, and agricultural exports.

Ireland has a temperate maritime climate, characterized by mild temperatures, abundant rainfall, and frequent cloud cover. The influence of the Atlantic Ocean moderates temperatures throughout the year, resulting in relatively mild winters and cool summers.

Winter temperatures typically range from 4°C to 7°C (39°F to 45°F) in coastal areas, with occasional frosts and snowfall in inland regions. Summers are cool and pleasant, with temperatures averaging between 14°C and 18°C (57°F to 64°F). However, temperatures can occasionally rise above 25°C (77°F) during heatwaves in summer.

Rainfall is a prominent feature of Ireland's climate, with precipitation occurring throughout the year. The western and northwestern regions receive the highest rainfall, while the east and southeast tend to be drier. The wettest months are typically October and November, while the driest months are April and May.

The weather in Ireland can be changeable and unpredictable, with rapid shifts between sunshine, rain, and clouds in a single day. This variability contributes to the country's lush green landscapes and is often celebrated in Irish culture through music, literature, and folklore.

Overall, Ireland's geography and climate combine to create a captivating environment characterized by stunning natural beauty, vibrant landscapes, and a unique cultural heritage that continues to enchant visitors from around the world.

History and Culture

Ireland boasts a rich and complex history that spans thousands of years, marked by ancient civilizations, invasions, cultural exchanges, and struggles for independence. Here's a glimpse into Ireland's fascinating historical journey:

Ancient Ireland
The island of Ireland has been inhabited for over 10,000 years, with evidence of early settlements dating back to the Mesolithic period. The Neolithic

period saw the construction of impressive megalithic monuments such as Newgrange and Knowth, showcasing Ireland's ancient architectural and engineering prowess.

Celtic Ireland
Around 500 BCE, Celtic tribes migrated to Ireland, bringing with them their language, art, and customs. The Celts established a sophisticated society characterized by tribal kingships, intricate artwork, and a rich oral tradition of mythology and storytelling.

Christianity
 In the 5th century CE, Christianity arrived in Ireland with the mission of Saint Patrick, who is credited with converting the Irish to Christianity. Monastic settlements flourished across the island, producing illuminated manuscripts like the Book of Kells and contributing to Ireland's reputation as a center of learning and spirituality during the Dark Ages.

Viking Invasions
From the 8th to the 11th centuries, Ireland experienced repeated Viking raids and invasions, leading to the establishment of Norse settlements

along the coast. The Vikings played a significant role in shaping Ireland's urban centers, trade networks, and political landscape.

Norman Conquest
In 1169, the Anglo-Norman invasion of Ireland began, marking the beginning of centuries of English influence and colonization. The Normans established feudal lordships, built castles, and introduced new legal and administrative systems, fundamentally altering Irish society.

Colonialism and Struggle for Independence
The 16th and 17th centuries witnessed English colonization and the imposition of harsh penal laws aimed at suppressing Irish culture and Catholicism. Centuries of resistance culminated in the Easter Rising of 1916 and the subsequent War of Independence, leading to the establishment of the Irish Free State in 1922.

Modern Ireland
Since gaining independence, Ireland has undergone significant social, economic, and cultural transformation. The country has embraced its cultural heritage while modernizing its economy and society, becoming known for its thriving arts

scene, literary tradition, and vibrant music and dance culture.

Ireland's culture is as diverse and dynamic as its history, shaped by centuries of tradition, innovation, and resilience. Here are some key aspects of Irish culture:

Literature
Ireland boasts a rich literary heritage, with renowned writers such as James Joyce, W.B. Yeats, Oscar Wilde, and Samuel Beckett making significant contributions to world literature. The country's literary tradition continues to thrive, with contemporary authors like Colm Tóibín, Anne Enright, and Sally Rooney gaining international acclaim.

Music and Dance
Music is an integral part of Irish culture, with traditional Irish music characterized by instruments such as the fiddle, tin whistle, bodhrán, and uilleann pipes. Irish dance, including step dancing and céilí dancing, is renowned for its intricate footwork and lively rhythms, showcased in performances worldwide.

Language
The Irish language, known as Irish or Gaelic (Gaeilge), holds a special place in Irish culture, serving as a symbol of national identity and heritage. While English is the predominant language spoken in Ireland today, efforts to promote and preserve the Irish language continue through education, media, and cultural initiatives.

Festivals and Celebrations
Ireland is renowned for its festive spirit, with a calendar full of cultural events, festivals, and celebrations. From St. Patrick's Day festivities to traditional music festivals like Fleadh Cheoil and literary events like the Dublin Writers Festival, there's always something to celebrate in Ireland.

Hospitality and Community
Irish hospitality is legendary, with locals known for their warmth, friendliness, and willingness to welcome visitors with open arms. Community spirit is strong in Ireland, with a tradition of coming together for music sessions, storytelling, and communal gatherings known as céilís.

The history and culture of Ireland are woven into the fabric of daily life, shaping the country's identity, values, and sense of belonging. Whether exploring ancient archaeological sites, attending a traditional music session, or savoring a pint of Guinness in a local pub, visitors to Ireland are sure to be captivated by the depth and richness of its cultural heritage.

Language and Etiquette

The official languages of Ireland are Irish (Gaeilge) and English, with English being the predominant language spoken throughout the country. However, Irish holds a special place in Irish culture and is recognized as an official language of the European Union. Here's a closer look at language and etiquette in Ireland:

Irish Language (Gaeilge)
Irish is a Celtic language with a rich linguistic heritage and is spoken as a first language by a small percentage of the population, primarily in Gaeltacht regions along the western coast. While most Irish people are bilingual and have some knowledge of Irish, English is the primary language of

communication in everyday life, business, and education.

English Language
English is the most widely spoken language in Ireland, used in government, media, education, and commerce. Visitors to Ireland will find that English is the language of choice for communication, and proficiency in English is essential for navigating daily interactions.

Irish culture places a strong emphasis on hospitality, politeness, and respect for others. Observing social etiquette and cultural customs can enhance your experience and help you connect with locals on a deeper level. Here are some etiquette tips for navigating social interactions in Ireland:

Greetings
When meeting someone for the first time, a firm handshake and direct eye contact are appropriate. In informal settings, a friendly "hello" or "how are you?" is common, followed by polite small talk.

Courtesy and Politeness
Irish people value courtesy and politeness in social interactions. It's customary to use "please," "thank you," and "excuse me" when speaking to others, whether in shops, restaurants, or public spaces.

Respect for Personal Space
While Irish people are generally friendly and outgoing, they also respect personal space and boundaries. Avoid standing too close or invading someone's personal space, especially with strangers.

Punctuality
 In social situations, punctuality is appreciated but not always strictly adhered to. Irish people tend to have a relaxed attitude toward time, so it's acceptable to be fashionably late for informal gatherings. However, punctuality is more important in business and formal settings.

Dining Etiquette
When dining out, it's customary to wait to be seated and to offer to pay your share of the bill when dining with others. Table manners are similar to those in other Western countries, with utensils used from the outside in and napkins placed on the lap.

Pub Etiquette
Pubs are an integral part of Irish social life, and
observing pub etiquette is essential. When entering
a pub, it's customary to wait to be served at the bar
rather than flagging down a bartender. Rounds of
drinks are common, with each person taking turns
buying drinks for the group.

By respecting the language and etiquette of Ireland,
visitors can immerse themselves in the country's
culture, forge meaningful connections with locals,
and create memorable experiences during their
time in the Emerald Isle.

Currency and Money Matters

The official currency of Ireland is the Euro (€),
abbreviated as EUR. The Euro is used for all
financial transactions, including purchases,
payments, and banking operations, throughout the
Republic of Ireland. Northern Ireland, as part of the
United Kingdom, uses the British Pound Sterling
(£).

Banknotes and Coins
The Euro is available in banknotes and coins of various denominations, each featuring distinct designs and security features. Banknotes come in denominations of €5, €10, €20, €50, €100, €200, and €500, while coins are available in denominations of 1 cent, 2 cents, 5 cents, 10 cents, 20 cents, 50 cents, €1, and €2.

Exchanging Currency
Foreign visitors to Ireland can exchange currency at banks, currency exchange offices, and some hotels and airports. It's advisable to compare exchange rates and fees before exchanging currency to ensure you get the best value for your money. Major credit and debit cards are widely accepted in Ireland, particularly in urban areas and tourist destinations, making it convenient to access funds without exchanging large amounts of cash.

ATMs
ATMs, known as "cash machines" or "bank machines," are readily available throughout Ireland and offer a convenient way to withdraw cash in the local currency. Most ATMs accept major international debit and credit cards, including Visa, Mastercard, and American Express. Be aware that

some ATMs may charge withdrawal fees, and it's advisable to inform your bank of your travel plans to avoid card issues or security concerns.

Credit and Debit Cards
Credit and debit cards are widely accepted in Ireland, particularly in hotels, restaurants, shops, and tourist attractions. Visa and Mastercard are the most commonly accepted card networks, followed by American Express and Discover. Contactless payment technology is prevalent in Ireland, allowing for quick and convenient transactions for small purchases.

Tipping
Tipping is not mandatory in Ireland but is appreciated for good service. In restaurants, a service charge may be included in the bill, in which case additional tipping is optional. If a service charge is not included, a tip of 10-15% of the total bill is customary for good service. Tipping for other services, such as taxi rides, hotel staff, and tour guides, is also discretionary but appreciated for exceptional service.

Safety and Security
Ireland is a relatively safe destination for travelers, but it's essential to take precautions to protect your money and valuables. Keep your cash, cards, and important documents secure at all times, and be cautious when using ATMs, especially in busy or touristy areas. It's advisable to carry a mix of cash and cards for flexibility and to inform your bank of your travel plans to prevent any issues with card transactions abroad.

By understanding currency and money matters in Ireland, travelers can navigate financial transactions with ease and make the most of their visit to the Emerald Isle. Whether exploring historic sites, enjoying traditional music in a cozy pub, or savoring the flavors of Irish cuisine, having the right currency and payment methods ensures a seamless and enjoyable travel experience.

Chapter 3. Regions of Ireland

Dublin and the East

Dublin, the vibrant capital city of Ireland, serves as a gateway to the rich cultural heritage, stunning landscapes, and historical landmarks of the eastern region.

Dublin
Dublin is a bustling metropolis renowned for its lively atmosphere, friendly locals, and wealth of attractions. Visitors to Dublin can explore a diverse array of experiences, from historic sites and museums to bustling markets and lively pubs. Here are some highlights of what Dublin has to offer:

Historical Landmarks
Dublin is steeped in history, with iconic landmarks such as Dublin Castle, Christ Church Cathedral, and St. Patrick's Cathedral showcasing the city's medieval heritage. Trinity College, home to the Book of Kells and the Long Room library, is a

must-visit for history buffs and literature enthusiasts alike.

Cultural Institutions
Dublin boasts a vibrant arts and culture scene, with world-class museums, galleries, and theaters. The National Museum of Ireland, the National Gallery of Ireland, and the Irish Museum of Modern Art (IMMA) offer insights into Ireland's rich artistic and cultural heritage. The Abbey Theatre, Ireland's national theater, showcases innovative performances and contemporary Irish playwrights.

Shopping and Dining
Dublin is a shopper's paradise, with a mix of high-end boutiques, quirky markets, and bustling shopping streets. Grafton Street and Henry Street are popular shopping destinations, while Temple Bar offers a vibrant mix of cafes, restaurants, and nightlife venues. Don't miss the chance to sample traditional Irish cuisine in Dublin's cozy pubs and award-winning restaurants.

Parks and Gardens
Dublin is known for its green spaces, with parks and gardens providing tranquil retreats from the hustle and bustle of city life. Phoenix Park, one of

Europe's largest urban parks, offers acres of open space, walking trails, and historic landmarks such as Áras an Uachtaráin, the official residence of the President of Ireland.

The East of Ireland

Beyond Dublin, the eastern region of Ireland is home to a wealth of natural beauty, historic sites, and charming towns and villages. From picturesque coastal towns to lush countryside, the East of Ireland offers a diverse range of experiences for visitors to explore.

Wicklow Mountains
Just south of Dublin, the Wicklow Mountains National Park offers stunning scenery, rugged landscapes, and outdoor adventures. Visitors can explore hiking trails, scenic drives, and historic sites such as Glendalough, an ancient monastic settlement nestled in a picturesque valley.

Coastal Towns
The East Coast of Ireland is dotted with charming coastal towns and villages, each offering its own unique charm and attractions. Places like Howth, Malahide, and Dun Laoghaire are popular day trip

destinations from Dublin, offering opportunities for seaside walks, fresh seafood, and panoramic views of the Irish Sea.

Historic Sites
The East of Ireland is rich in history, with ancient ruins, castles, and historic estates waiting to be explored. Newgrange, a UNESCO World Heritage Site, is one of Ireland's most important prehistoric monuments, while Powerscourt Estate and Gardens offer a glimpse into Ireland's aristocratic past.

Gardens and Estates
The East of Ireland is home to a wealth of stunning gardens and estates, where visitors can stroll through manicured gardens, admire historic architecture, and enjoy afternoon tea. Powerscourt Gardens, Mount Usher Gardens, and the National Botanic Gardens are just a few of the region's horticultural gems.

From the vibrant streets of Dublin to the scenic beauty of the Wicklow Mountains and the charming coastal towns along the East Coast, Dublin and the East of Ireland offer a wealth of experiences waiting to be discovered. Whether exploring historic landmarks, enjoying outdoor adventures, or savoring the flavors of Irish cuisine, this region promises unforgettable memories for visitors of all ages.

Cork and the South

Cork, Ireland's second-largest city, serves as a gateway to the picturesque landscapes, charming towns, and cultural attractions of the southern region.

Cork
Cork City, affectionately known as the "Rebel County," is a vibrant hub of culture, history, and innovation. With its lively atmosphere, friendly locals, and stunning riverfront setting, Cork offers visitors a memorable blend of urban excitement and natural beauty. Here are some highlights of what Cork City has to offer:

Historic Landmarks
Cork boasts a wealth of historic landmarks, including the iconic Cork City Gaol, a former prison turned museum that offers insight into Ireland's turbulent past. St. Fin Barre's Cathedral, Crawford

Art Gallery, and Elizabeth Fort are other notable landmarks that showcase Cork's rich heritage.

Cultural Institutions

Cork is renowned for its thriving arts and cultural scene, with a diverse array of galleries, theaters, and performance venues. The Cork Opera House hosts a variety of concerts, plays, and musical performances, while the Glucksman Gallery and Cork Public Museum offer exhibitions that celebrate the city's artistic and historical heritage.

Shopping and Dining

Cork is a paradise for foodies and shoppers alike, with a vibrant culinary scene and an eclectic mix of shops, markets, and boutiques. The English Market, one of Ireland's oldest municipal markets, is a must-visit destination for gourmet food products, fresh produce, and artisanal goods. Cork's bustling streets are lined with cafes, restaurants, and pubs serving everything from traditional Irish fare to international cuisine.

Parks and Gardens

Despite its urban setting, Cork is surrounded by lush greenery and scenic parks that provide tranquil escapes from the city bustle. Fitzgerald's Park, located along the banks of the River Lee, features beautiful gardens, walking paths, and the Cork Public Museum. The nearby University College Cork (UCC) campus is home to the historic Honan Chapel and picturesque grounds perfect for a leisurely stroll.

The South of Ireland

Beyond Cork City, the southern region of Ireland offers a treasure trove of natural beauty, historic sites, and cultural attractions. From rugged coastlines to verdant countryside, the South of Ireland beckons visitors to explore its scenic landscapes and vibrant communities. Here are some highlights of what the South of Ireland has to offer:

Ring of Kerry
The Ring of Kerry is one of Ireland's most iconic scenic drives, offering breathtaking views of rugged coastline, verdant hills, and picturesque villages. Along the route, visitors can explore historic sites like Ross Castle, admire natural wonders like the Gap of Dunloe, and soak in the stunning vistas of the Atlantic Ocean.

Killarney National Park
Located in County Kerry, Killarney National Park is a haven for outdoor enthusiasts, with pristine lakes, dense forests, and majestic mountains. Visitors can explore the park's network of hiking trails, cycle along scenic routes, or take a leisurely boat ride on the tranquil lakes of Killarney.

Historic Towns and Villages
The South of Ireland is dotted with charming towns and villages steeped in history and tradition. Places like Kinsale, Cobh, and Dingle are known for their colorful streets, historic architecture, and vibrant cultural scenes. Each town offers its own unique charm and attractions, from seafood festivals to traditional music sessions.

Gardens and Estates
The South of Ireland is home to a wealth of beautiful gardens and stately estates, where visitors can wander through manicured grounds, admire exotic plants, and learn about the region's horticultural heritage. Muckross House and Gardens, Bantry House and Gardens, and Blarney Castle and Gardens are just a few of the South's botanical gems.

From the bustling streets of Cork City to the scenic beauty of the Ring of Kerry and the historic charm of towns and villages throughout the region, Cork and the South of Ireland offer a diverse range of experiences waiting to be discovered. Whether exploring ancient landmarks, enjoying outdoor adventures, or savoring the flavors of Irish cuisine, this region promises unforgettable memories for visitors of all interests and ages.

Galway and the West

Galway, known as the "City of Tribes," serves as a vibrant gateway to the rugged beauty, cultural richness, and traditional charm of the western region of Ireland.

Galway

Nestled on the shores of Galway Bay, Galway City is a lively cultural hub renowned for its vibrant arts scene, historic landmarks, and welcoming atmosphere. With its bustling streets, lively pubs, and picturesque waterfront, Galway offers visitors a taste of authentic Irish hospitality and charm. Here are some highlights of what Galway City has to offer:

Medieval Streets
Galway's medieval city center is a maze of narrow streets, colorful facades, and historic buildings that exude old-world charm. Visitors can wander along cobbled lanes like Quay Street and Shop Street, browse artisan shops and boutiques, and soak in the vibrant atmosphere of this bustling urban hub.

Cultural Institutions
Galway is a cultural powerhouse, with a wealth of galleries, theaters, and performance venues showcasing the best of Irish arts and culture. The Galway City Museum offers insights into the city's rich history and heritage, while the Druid Theatre Company presents innovative productions of contemporary and classic plays.

Music and Festivals
Galway is renowned for its lively music scene and vibrant festival culture, with traditional Irish music sessions taking place in pubs and venues throughout the city. The Galway International Arts Festival, Galway Film Fleadh, and Galway Oyster

Festival are just a few of the annual events that draw visitors from around the world.

Galway Bay and the Claddagh
Galway's picturesque waterfront is a focal point of the city, with stunning views of Galway Bay and the iconic Claddagh neighborhood. Visitors can stroll along the promenade, enjoy a boat cruise on the bay, or explore the historic Claddagh district, known for its traditional fishing village charm.

The West of Ireland

Beyond Galway City, the western region of Ireland is a land of rugged beauty, ancient history, and breathtaking landscapes. From the dramatic cliffs of the Wild Atlantic Way to the tranquil beauty of Connemara National Park, the West of Ireland beckons visitors to explore its diverse natural wonders and cultural treasures. Here are some highlights of what the West of Ireland has to offer:

The Wild Atlantic Way
The West of Ireland is home to some of the most stunning coastal scenery in Europe, with the Wild Atlantic Way offering a breathtaking journey along

the rugged coastline. Visitors can explore dramatic cliffs, hidden coves, and picturesque seaside villages as they travel along this iconic coastal route.

Connemara National Park
 Located just a short drive from Galway City, Connemara National Park is a wilderness oasis of mountains, bogs, and lakes. Visitors can hike along scenic trails, spot native wildlife such as red deer and Connemara ponies, and take in panoramic views of the rugged landscape.

Aran Islands
 Just off the coast of Galway Bay, the Aran Islands offer a glimpse into traditional Irish island life. Visitors can explore ancient stone forts, cycle along scenic coastal roads, and immerse themselves in the unique culture and language of these remote island communities.

Historic Sites
The West of Ireland is rich in history and heritage, with ancient monuments, medieval castles, and historic estates waiting to be explored. Kylemore Abbey, Dunguaire Castle, and the Poulnabrone Dolmen are just a few of the region's iconic

landmarks that offer insights into Ireland's storied past.

From the lively streets of Galway City to the rugged beauty of the Wild Atlantic Way and the ancient heritage of the Aran Islands, Galway and the West of Ireland offer a wealth of experiences waiting to be discovered. Whether exploring historic landmarks, enjoying outdoor adventures, or savoring the flavors of traditional Irish cuisine, this region promises unforgettable memories for visitors of all interests and ages.

Belfast and Northern Ireland

Belfast, the vibrant capital of Northern Ireland, serves as a gateway to the stunning landscapes, rich history, and cultural attractions of the western region of the country.

Belfast

Nestled along the banks of the River Lagan, Belfast is a dynamic city with a fascinating history, vibrant arts scene, and warm hospitality. From its historic landmarks and bustling markets to its lively pubs and thriving cultural institutions, Belfast offers visitors a captivating blend of old-world charm and modern sophistication. Here are some highlights of what Belfast has to offer:

Historical Landmarks
Belfast is steeped in history, with iconic landmarks such as Belfast City Hall, Titanic Belfast, and the Crumlin Road Gaol showcasing the city's rich heritage. The murals of West Belfast, which depict the city's troubled past and ongoing quest for peace, offer poignant insights into Northern Ireland's complex history.

Cultural Institutions
Belfast boasts a vibrant arts and cultural scene, with world-class museums, galleries, and theaters that celebrate the city's artistic heritage. The Ulster Museum, the MAC (Metropolitan Arts Centre), and the Grand Opera House are just a few of the cultural institutions that offer exhibitions, performances, and events for visitors to enjoy.

Shopping and Dining
Belfast is a shopper's paradise, with a diverse range of shops, markets, and boutiques offering everything from high-end fashion to locally-made

crafts and artisanal goods. St. George's Market, one of the oldest markets in Ireland, is a must-visit destination for gourmet food products, fresh produce, and handmade crafts. Belfast's vibrant dining scene offers a tantalizing array of culinary delights, from traditional Irish fare to international cuisine.

Parks and Gardens
 Despite its urban setting, Belfast is surrounded by green spaces and scenic parks that provide tranquil escapes from the city bustle. Botanic Gardens, located in the heart of the city, features beautiful gardens, tropical greenhouses, and the historic Palm House. Cave Hill Country Park, just north of the city, offers stunning views of Belfast and the surrounding countryside.

The West of Ireland

Beyond Belfast, the western region of Ireland is a land of rugged beauty, ancient history, and breathtaking landscapes. From the dramatic cliffs of the Wild Atlantic Way to the lush greenery of Connemara, the West of Ireland beckons visitors to explore its diverse natural wonders and cultural treasures. Here are some highlights of what the West of Ireland has to offer:

The Wild Atlantic Way
The West of Ireland is home to some of the most stunning coastal scenery in Europe, with the Wild Atlantic Way offering a breathtaking journey along the rugged coastline. Visitors can explore dramatic cliffs, hidden coves, and picturesque seaside villages as they travel along this iconic coastal route.

Connemara
Located in County Galway, Connemara is a wilderness oasis of mountains, bogs, and lakes that offers a tranquil retreat from the hustle and bustle of city life. Visitors can explore scenic hiking trails, spot native wildlife such as Connemara ponies and red deer, and immerse themselves in the region's rich Gaelic culture.

Achill Island
Just off the coast of County Mayo, Achill Island is the largest island off the coast of Ireland and offers a unique blend of natural beauty and cultural heritage. Visitors can explore sandy beaches, rugged cliffs, and ancient ruins, or enjoy outdoor activities such as hiking, cycling, and water sports.

Historic Sites
The West of Ireland is rich in history and heritage, with ancient monuments, medieval castles, and historic estates waiting to be explored. Kylemore Abbey, Westport House, and the Ceide Fields are just a few of the region's iconic landmarks that offer insights into Ireland's storied past.

From the vibrant streets of Belfast to the rugged beauty of the Wild Atlantic Way and the ancient heritage of Connemara, Belfast and the West of Ireland offer a wealth of experiences waiting to be discovered. Whether exploring historic landmarks, enjoying outdoor adventures, or savoring the flavors of traditional Irish cuisine, this region promises unforgettable memories for visitors of all interests and ages.

58

Chapter 4. Top Attractions

Historical Sites and Landmarks

Ireland's landscape is adorned with a tapestry of historical sites and landmarks, each weaving a story of the country's rich cultural heritage. Here's a glimpse into some of the most captivating:

Newgrange
 Nestled in County Meath, Newgrange is a testament to the ingenuity of Ireland's ancient inhabitants, predating both Stonehenge and the Egyptian pyramids. This Neolithic passage tomb showcases advanced architectural prowess.

Rock of Cashel
Perched atop a limestone hill in County Tipperary, the Rock of Cashel boasts medieval structures like cathedrals and round towers. With a backdrop of myth and legend, it offers panoramic views of the surrounding countryside.

Cliffs of Moher

Stretching along County Clare's Atlantic coast, the Cliffs of Moher stand as imposing sentinels, rising dramatically from the ocean. Their rugged beauty and awe-inspiring vistas make them a must-visit for nature enthusiasts.

Blarney Castle

Near Cork City, Blarney Castle invites visitors to kiss the legendary Blarney Stone for eloquence. Surrounded by verdant gardens and woodland trails, it's steeped in Irish folklore and charm.

Giant's Causeway

Along County Antrim's coast, the Giant's Causeway is a marvel of nature, with hexagonal basalt columns formed by ancient volcanic activity. Myth and legend shroud this UNESCO World Heritage Site, adding to its allure.

Kilmainham Gaol

In Dublin, Kilmainham Gaol serves as a poignant reminder of Ireland's struggle for independence. Its stark cells and corridors bear witness to the imprisonment and execution of political prisoners.

The Book of Kells
 Housed in Trinity College Library, the Book of Kells is a masterpiece of medieval artistry, renowned for its intricate designs and vibrant colors. Dating back to the 9th century, it remains a prized cultural treasure.

Bunratty Castle and Folk Park
Located in County Clare, Bunratty Castle offers a glimpse into medieval life, while its Folk Park recreates 19th-century rural Ireland. Visitors can immerse themselves in traditional music, storytelling, and crafts.

These sites, among many others, stand as pillars of Ireland's history and heritage, inviting visitors to delve into the country's rich tapestry of culture and tradition.

Natural Wonders

Ireland's landscape is a tapestry of stunning natural wonders, from rugged coastlines and towering cliffs to verdant valleys and serene lakes. Here's a glimpse into some of the most breathtaking natural attractions the country has to offer:

The Cliffs of Moher
Rising majestically from the Atlantic Ocean along
County Clare's coast, the Cliffs of Moher are one of
Ireland's most iconic natural landmarks. With sheer
cliffs reaching heights of up to 214 meters, these
dramatic cliffs offer awe-inspiring views of the
rugged coastline and the endless expanse of the
Atlantic horizon.

The Giant's Causeway
Along the rugged coast of County Antrim in
Northern Ireland, the Giant's Causeway is a
geological marvel composed of thousands of
interlocking basalt columns formed by ancient
volcanic activity. Steeped in myth and legend, this
UNESCO World Heritage Site offers visitors a
glimpse into Ireland's ancient past and a landscape
unlike any other.

Connemara National Park
Nestled in the heart of County Galway, Connemara
National Park is a wilderness oasis of rugged
mountains, pristine lakes, and vast expanses of
bogland. With a network of scenic hiking trails,
visitors can explore this untouched landscape and

encounter native wildlife such as Connemara
ponies, red deer, and golden eagles.

The Ring of Kerry
Meandering along the scenic coastline of County
Kerry, the Ring of Kerry is a picturesque driving
route that showcases some of Ireland's most
breathtaking scenery. From rugged cliffs and sandy
beaches to rolling hills and charming villages, the
Ring of Kerry offers endless opportunities for
exploration and discovery.

The Burren
Located in County Clare, the Burren is a unique
limestone landscape characterized by its rugged
terrain, barren hills, and ancient stone formations.
Despite its harsh appearance, the Burren is home to
a diverse array of flora and fauna, including rare
wildflowers and orchids that thrive in its rocky
crevices.

Skellig Michael
Rising dramatically from the Atlantic Ocean off the
coast of County Kerry, Skellig Michael is a remote
island that holds a special place in Irish history and
mythology. Home to an ancient monastery dating
back to the 6th century, this UNESCO World

Heritage Site offers visitors a glimpse into the lives of early Christian monks and breathtaking views of the surrounding seascape.

The Dark Hedges
Tucked away in County Antrim, the Dark Hedges is a mystical avenue of beech trees that create a hauntingly beautiful canopy over a quiet country road. Made famous by its appearance in the television series "Game of Thrones," the Dark Hedges enchant visitors with their otherworldly beauty and timeless charm.

These natural wonders, among many others, showcase the diversity and beauty of Ireland's landscape, inviting visitors to explore and connect with the country's rich natural heritage. Whether hiking along rugged cliffs, driving through picturesque valleys, or simply soaking in the serenity of a tranquil lake, Ireland's natural wonders offer endless opportunities for adventure and discovery.

Museums and Galleries

Ireland boasts a plethora of museums and galleries, each offering a unique glimpse into the country's rich history, culture, and artistic expression. Here's a selection of notable institutions spread across the Emerald Isle:

National Museum of Ireland (Dublin)
With branches in Dublin and beyond, the National Museum of Ireland is a treasure trove of archaeological, historical, and natural wonders. Visitors can marvel at ancient artifacts, including the Ardagh Chalice and the Tara Brooch, and explore exhibitions that span from prehistoric times to the modern era.

Irish Museum of Modern Art (IMMA) (Dublin)
Housed in the historic Royal Hospital Kilmainham, IMMA is the epicenter of contemporary art in Ireland. Its diverse collection and rotating exhibitions showcase the latest trends and innovative works by Irish and international artists.

National Gallery of Ireland (Dublin)
Situated in Dublin's city center, the National Gallery boasts an impressive collection of European and Irish art, spanning from the Middle Ages to the

present day. Visitors can admire works by renowned artists and immerse themselves in the rich cultural tapestry of Ireland.

Trinity College Library (Dublin)
Home to the legendary Book of Kells, Trinity College Library is a bibliophile's dream. Its Long Room, adorned with antique books and busts of famous scholars, offers a glimpse into the past and showcases the beauty of Ireland's literary heritage.

Ulster Museum (Belfast)
Nestled in Belfast's Botanic Gardens, the Ulster Museum is a cultural hub that celebrates Northern Ireland's heritage. From natural history exhibits to contemporary art installations, the museum offers something for everyone.

Chester Beatty (Dublin)
Tucked away in Dublin Castle, the Chester Beatty Library houses an extraordinary collection of manuscripts, prints, and artifacts from around the world. Visitors can explore the diverse cultures and artistic traditions that shape our global heritage.

Crawford Art Gallery (Cork)
Located in Cork City, the Crawford Art Gallery
showcases the best of Irish and European art. Its
collection spans centuries and includes works by
renowned artists as well as emerging talents,
providing a comprehensive overview of artistic
expression.

Galway City Museum (Galway)
 Situated on the banks of the River Corrib, the
Galway City Museum offers a window into the city's
past and present. From archaeological finds to
contemporary exhibitions, the museum celebrates
Galway's vibrant culture and history.

These museums and galleries, scattered across
Ireland's cities and countryside, offer visitors a
chance to delve into the country's multifaceted
identity and artistic legacy. Whether exploring
ancient relics, admiring masterpieces, or
discovering contemporary trends, Ireland's cultural
institutions provide endless opportunities for
inspiration and discovery.

Festivals and Events

Ireland is renowned for its vibrant festival culture, with events celebrating everything from music and literature to food and folklore.

St. Patrick's Festival
Held annually on March 17th, St. Patrick's Festival is a nationwide celebration of Ireland's patron saint and cultural heritage. From colorful parades and street performances to traditional music sessions and Irish dancing, the festival showcases the best of Irish culture and hospitality.

Galway International Arts Festival
Taking place each July in Galway City, the Galway International Arts Festival is one of Ireland's premier cultural events. Featuring a diverse program of music, theater, visual arts, and street performances, the festival transforms the city into a vibrant hub of creativity and innovation.

Electric Picnic
Held annually in Stradbally, County Laois, Electric Picnic is Ireland's largest music and arts festival. With multiple stages featuring an eclectic lineup of musicians and performers, as well as art installations, workshops, and gourmet food stalls,

Electric Picnic offers an unforgettable weekend of entertainment and exploration.

All-Ireland Fleadh Cheoil
The All-Ireland Fleadh Cheoil is the largest traditional Irish music festival in the world, attracting thousands of musicians and enthusiasts from across Ireland and beyond. Held annually in different locations, the festival features competitions, concerts, workshops, and sessions celebrating the rich heritage of Irish music and dance.

Dublin Horse Show
Held each August at the Royal Dublin Society (RDS) showgrounds, the Dublin Horse Show is one of Ireland's most prestigious equestrian events. Featuring showjumping competitions, dressage displays, and equestrian entertainment, the Dublin Horse Show attracts riders, breeders, and spectators from around the globe.

Dublin International Film Festival
The Dublin International Film Festival is Ireland's premier film event, showcasing the best of Irish and international cinema. Held annually in February, the festival features screenings, premieres, Q&A

sessions with filmmakers, and special events celebrating the art of filmmaking.

Galway Oyster Festival
Taking place each September in Galway City, the Galway Oyster Festival is a celebration of Ireland's culinary heritage and seafood culture. From oyster shucking competitions and gourmet tastings to live music and entertainment, the festival offers a feast for the senses.

Kilkenny Arts Festival
Held annually in Kilkenny City, the Kilkenny Arts Festival is a multidisciplinary event that celebrates the best of Irish and international arts and culture. From classical music concerts and theater productions to literary readings and visual arts exhibitions, the festival offers a diverse program of events for all ages and interests.

These festivals and events, among many others throughout the year, showcase the diversity and creativity of Ireland's cultural scene. Whether attending a traditional music session, exploring contemporary art installations, or indulging in gourmet cuisine, Ireland's festivals offer unforgettable experiences for visitors and locals alike.

Chapter 5. Activities and Adventures

Hiking and Outdoor Activities

Ireland's diverse landscapes, ranging from rugged mountains to picturesque coastlines, provide a rich tapestry for outdoor enthusiasts to explore.

Venture along the Wicklow Way, tracing through County Wicklow's verdant hills and ancient forests, or immerse yourself in the panoramic views along the Kerry Way as it winds around the stunning Iveragh Peninsula. Discover the geological wonders of the Causeway Coast Way in County Antrim, where dramatic cliffs and rock formations await. Connemara National Park in County Galway offers a haven for hikers with its network of trails through mountains, bogs, and lakes, while the Burren Way in County Clare unveils the surreal beauty of its limestone landscape, dotted with ancient ruins and wildflowers.

For thrill-seekers, Ireland's Atlantic coast beckons with world-class surfing spots in County Donegal and County Clare, where waves roll in with consistent swells. Cyclists can pedal along scenic routes like the Great Western Greenway in County Mayo or the Ring of Kerry in County Kerry, passing through quaint villages and stunning landscapes. Kayakers can explore hidden coves and sea caves along the coastline, while rock climbers can tackle challenging crags and cliffs scattered across the country. And for those seeking a more leisurely adventure, horseback riding through Ireland's rolling countryside offers a tranquil way to soak in the scenery and connect with nature.

From the serene tranquility of a leisurely hike to the adrenaline rush of surfing towering waves, Ireland's outdoor offerings cater to adventurers of all levels and interests. So, whether you're seeking a peaceful retreat amidst nature's embrace or an exhilarating outdoor escapade, the Emerald Isle invites you to discover its boundless beauty and endless possibilities for adventure.

Water Sports

With its rugged coastline, pristine lakes, and meandering rivers, Ireland offers a playground for water sports enthusiasts of all kinds. From thrilling surfing sessions along the Atlantic coast to tranquil kayaking excursions on scenic lakes, the Emerald

Isle provides endless opportunities for aquatic adventure. Here's a comprehensive guide to water sports in Ireland:

Surfing
Ireland's Atlantic coastline is renowned for its world-class surf breaks, attracting surfers from around the globe. From the towering waves of County Donegal's Bundoran to the consistent swells of County Clare's Lahinch, there's something for surfers of all levels. Other popular surfing spots include County Sligo's Strandhill, County Kerry's Inch Beach, and County Mayo's Achill Island, each offering a unique surfing experience amidst breathtaking coastal scenery.

Kayaking
Exploring Ireland's waterways by kayak is a serene and immersive way to experience the country's natural beauty. Paddle along tranquil lakes like Lough Corrib in County Galway or Lough Erne in County Fermanagh, where you can admire scenic landscapes and spot native wildlife. For a more adventurous experience, sea kayaking along the rugged coastline of County Kerry or County Cork offers the chance to explore hidden coves, sea caves, and remote islands.

Stand-Up Paddleboarding (SUP)
Stand-up paddleboarding has become increasingly popular in Ireland, offering a unique way to explore the country's waterways while enjoying a full-body workout. Try SUP along the River Shannon, Ireland's longest river, or navigate through the scenic water channels of County Kerry's Dingle Peninsula. With calm lakes, rivers, and coastal waters to choose from, SUP enthusiasts can enjoy peaceful paddling or take on the challenge of riding waves in the open sea.

Windsurfing and Kitesurfing
For those seeking adrenaline-fueled thrills, windsurfing and kitesurfing provide an exhilarating experience on Ireland's windy coasts. Head to County Kerry's Brandon Bay, known as one of the best windsurfing spots in Europe, or catch the strong winds and rolling waves of County Sligo's Mullaghmore. Kitesurfers will find ideal conditions in County Mayo's Achill Island, where steady winds and expansive beaches create the perfect playground for catching air.

Sailing and Boating
With its numerous lakes, rivers, and coastal harbors, Ireland offers ample opportunities for sailing and boating enthusiasts to take to the water. Explore the tranquil waters of Lough Neagh in Northern Ireland, the largest freshwater lake in the British Isles, or set sail along the scenic coastline of County Cork's West Cork Peninsula. From leisurely cruises to competitive regattas, there's no shortage of ways to enjoy Ireland's maritime heritage.

Fishing
Ireland's rivers and lakes are renowned for their abundance of fish, making it a popular destination for anglers seeking a rewarding fishing experience. Cast your line in the renowned trout and salmon waters of County Mayo's Lough Mask or County Kerry's River Laune, or try your hand at sea angling along the rugged coastline of County Donegal or County Cork. Whether fly fishing in pristine rivers or deep-sea fishing in the open ocean, Ireland offers a diverse range of fishing opportunities for anglers of all skill levels.

From the adrenaline rush of surfing and kitesurfing to the serene tranquility of kayaking and fishing, water sports enthusiasts will find plenty to explore and enjoy in Ireland's waters. With its stunning natural landscapes and welcoming coastal communities, the Emerald Isle invites visitors to dive in and experience the thrill of aquatic adventure firsthand.

Golfing

Ireland is renowned worldwide as a premier destination for golf enthusiasts, offering a wealth of championship courses, stunning landscapes, and a rich golfing heritage.

Championship Courses
Ireland boasts some of the world's most prestigious championship golf courses, many of which have hosted major tournaments and attracted top players from around the globe. From the legendary links courses of the rugged west coast to the parkland gems of the east, golfers of all skill levels can find a course to challenge and inspire them.

Links Courses
Ireland's rugged coastline is home to some of the most iconic links courses in the world, characterized by undulating dunes, challenging winds, and breathtaking views of the Atlantic

Ocean. Courses like Ballybunion, Lahinch, and Royal County Down offer a true test of golfing skill and provide an unforgettable experience for players.

Parkland Courses
Inland, Ireland's parkland courses offer lush fairways, manicured greens, and scenic surroundings that provide a different but equally rewarding golfing experience. Courses such as The K Club, Adare Manor, and Druids Glen showcase the country's natural beauty and offer a more tranquil setting for golfers to enjoy.

Hidden Gems
Beyond the well-known championship courses, Ireland is also home to a myriad of hidden gems waiting to be discovered by golfing enthusiasts. From quaint nine-hole courses tucked away in the countryside to lesser-known links along the Wild Atlantic Way, these hidden gems offer unique challenges and a chance to explore the lesser-known corners of Ireland's golfing landscape.

Golfing Events
Throughout the year, Ireland plays host to a variety of golfing events and tournaments that attract

players and spectators alike. From professional tournaments like the Irish Open to amateur events and charity fundraisers, there's always something happening on the Irish golfing calendar.

Golfing Culture
Golf is deeply ingrained in Irish culture, with a rich tradition dating back centuries. The country is home to countless golf clubs and societies where players can enjoy camaraderie both on and off the course. The 19th hole—a term coined for the clubhouse bar—is a cherished tradition where golfers gather to recount their rounds, share stories, and enjoy a pint of Guinness or a dram of Irish whiskey.

Hospitality
Irish hospitality is legendary, and golfers visiting the country can expect a warm welcome at golf clubs and resorts across the land. From luxurious accommodations and world-class dining to friendly service and a relaxed atmosphere, Ireland's golfing establishments go above and beyond to ensure a memorable experience for every guest.

Golfing in Ireland is a truly exceptional experience, combining world-class courses, stunning scenery, rich history, and warm hospitality. Whether you're a seasoned pro or a casual player, a golfing trip to Ireland promises unforgettable moments on the fairways and memories to last a lifetime.

Cycling and Walking Tours

Ireland's picturesque landscapes, charming villages, and rich cultural heritage make it an ideal destination for cycling and walking enthusiasts. Whether you prefer leisurely rides through lush countryside or challenging treks along rugged coastlines, Ireland offers a plethora of opportunities to explore its beauty on two wheels or on foot.

Cycling Tours
Embark on a cycling adventure along the Great Western Greenway in County Mayo, a 42-kilometer route that follows the path of an old railway line, offering stunning views of Clew Bay and the surrounding mountains.
Pedal through the scenic Ring of Kerry in County Kerry, a 179-kilometer loop that takes you past majestic mountains, sparkling lakes, and charming villages, with plenty of opportunities to stop and explore along the way.

Explore the stunning landscapes of the Wild Atlantic Way, a 2,500-kilometer coastal route that stretches from Donegal in the north to Cork in the south, passing through rugged cliffs, sandy beaches, and picturesque seaside towns.

Cycle along the Waterford Greenway in County Waterford, a 46-kilometer trail that follows the route of an old railway line, offering panoramic views of the River Suir and passing through tunnels, viaducts, and quaint villages.

Join a guided cycling tour of the Aran Islands in County Galway, where you can explore ancient ruins, scenic beaches, and traditional Irish villages while soaking in the island's unique culture and heritage.

Walking Tours

Embark on a walking tour of the Cliffs of Moher in County Clare, where you can hike along the cliff-top trails and enjoy breathtaking views of the Atlantic Ocean and the Aran Islands.

Explore the scenic beauty of the Wicklow Mountains in County Wicklow on a guided walking tour, where you can trek through lush forests, past sparkling lakes, and up to panoramic viewpoints.

Discover the ancient history and natural wonders of the Burren in County Clare on a guided walking tour, where you can explore limestone pavements, hidden caves, and megalithic tombs dating back thousands of years.

Join a guided walking tour of the Causeway Coast in County Antrim, where you can hike along rugged cliffs, cross the iconic Carrick-a-Rede Rope Bridge, and marvel at the geological wonders of the Giant's Causeway.

Explore the vibrant streets and historic landmarks of Dublin on a guided walking tour of the city, where you can learn about its rich history, culture, and literary heritage from knowledgeable local guides.

Whether you choose to explore Ireland's stunning landscapes on two wheels or on foot, cycling and walking tours offer a unique way to experience the country's natural beauty, rich history, and vibrant culture. So grab your bike or lace up your hiking boots and get ready to discover the magic of Ireland at your own pace.

84

Chapter 6: Eating and Drinking

Traditional Irish Cuisine

Irish cuisine is a celebration of hearty, comforting dishes that reflect the country's agricultural heritage and culinary traditions passed down through generations.

Irish Stew
A warming dish made with tender chunks of lamb or beef, potatoes, onions, and carrots, simmered in a savory broth flavored with herbs like thyme and parsley. Served with crusty bread or soda bread, it's a comforting meal that's perfect for chilly days.

Boxty
Also known as "Irish potato pancakes," boxty is made from grated potatoes mixed with flour, baking soda, buttermilk, and sometimes eggs. Fried until golden and crispy, it's often served with sour cream or honey for a delicious treat.

Seafood Chowder
Made with a creamy broth, chunks of fish, shrimp, mussels, and smoked salmon, seafood chowder

showcases Ireland's abundant coastline and fresh seafood. Flavored with herbs, garlic, and white wine, it's a flavorful dish that's sure to impress.

Shepherd's Pie
A hearty dish made with minced lamb or beef, vegetables, and topped with creamy mashed potatoes. Baked until golden and bubbling, it's a classic comfort food that's perfect for sharing.

Soda Bread
A simple bread made with flour, baking soda, salt, and buttermilk, soda bread is a staple of Irish baking. Served warm with butter and jam, it's perfect for breakfast or as a side with soups and stews.

Irish Breakfast
A hearty meal consisting of bacon, sausages, black and white pudding, eggs, tomatoes, mushrooms, and baked beans. Served with toast or soda bread and a cup of tea or coffee, it's a filling way to start the day.

Barmbrack
A traditional fruitcake made with dried fruit soaked in tea, barmbrack is often enjoyed around

Halloween. Served with butter, it pairs perfectly
with a cup of tea or a glass of whiskey.

Guinness Beef Stew
A rich and flavorful stew made with chunks of beef,
onions, carrots, and potatoes, simmered in
Guinness stout. The stout adds depth and
complexity to the stew, making it a comforting and
indulgent dish.

These dishes, among others, form the backbone of
traditional Irish cuisine, offering a taste of Ireland's
rich culinary heritage and warm hospitality.
Whether enjoyed in a cozy pub or prepared at
home, traditional Irish fare is sure to delight your
taste buds and leave you feeling satisfied.

Pubs and Nightlife

Ireland's pubs are legendary, serving as the heart
and soul of social life in cities, towns, and villages
across the country. From traditional Irish pubs with
cozy fireplaces and live music sessions to modern
cocktail bars and bustling nightclubs, Ireland offers
a vibrant and diverse nightlife scene that caters to
all tastes and preferences.

Traditional Irish Pubs
Step into a traditional Irish pub and experience the warm hospitality and convivial atmosphere that has made them famous around the world. From historic taverns dating back centuries to cozy local pubs serving up pints of Guinness and hearty pub grub, Ireland's pub scene is steeped in tradition and charm. Look out for hidden gems like Sean's Bar in Athlone, Ireland's oldest pub, or The Brazen Head in Dublin, a favorite haunt of literary legends like James Joyce and Brendan Behan.

Live Music Sessions
No visit to Ireland is complete without experiencing the magic of a live music session in a local pub. From soulful ballads and lively jigs to foot-stomping reels and contemporary covers, Irish music is an integral part of the pub culture. Head to places like Matt Molloy's in Westport, where you can catch traditional Irish music sessions seven nights a week, or The Cobblestone in Dublin, a renowned venue for authentic Irish music and craic.

Craft Beer and Whiskey Bars
For beer enthusiasts and whiskey connoisseurs, Ireland offers a burgeoning craft beer and whiskey

scene with a growing number of specialty bars and microbreweries. Sample a diverse range of locally brewed beers and artisanal spirits at establishments like The Bierhaus in Cork, which boasts an extensive selection of craft beers from around the world, or The Dingle Whiskey Bar in Dublin, where you can savor rare and vintage whiskeys in a cozy setting.

Cocktail Bars and Speakeasies
For a taste of modern Irish nightlife, explore the burgeoning cocktail bar scene in cities like Dublin, Galway, and Belfast. From trendy rooftop bars and chic speakeasies to stylish cocktail lounges and hidden gems, Ireland's cities offer a diverse array of nightlife options for cocktail aficionados. Check out places like The Dead Rabbit in Belfast, named the World's Best Bar, or The Liquor Rooms in Dublin, known for its creative cocktails and vintage decor.

Nightclubs and Late-Night Venues
When the sun goes down, Ireland's cities come alive with a vibrant nightlife that caters to partygoers of all ages. Dance the night away at popular nightclubs like Coppers in Dublin, known for its lively atmosphere and late-night party scene, or Thompsons Garage in Belfast, a legendary venue for

electronic music and underground beats. Alternatively, head to cultural hubs like Galway's Latin Quarter, where you'll find a mix of traditional pubs, live music venues, and late-night eateries buzzing with energy.

From traditional Irish pubs to modern cocktail bars and bustling nightclubs, Ireland's nightlife offers something for everyone. Whether you're looking to soak up the atmosphere of a local pub session, sample craft beers and artisanal whiskeys, or dance until the early hours, Ireland invites you to experience its vibrant and dynamic nightlife scene firsthand.

Food Festivals

Ireland's culinary scene is celebrated through a diverse array of food festivals held throughout the year, showcasing the country's rich gastronomic heritage and vibrant food culture. From traditional Irish fare to international cuisines, these festivals offer a feast for the senses and a chance to indulge in delicious dishes, artisanal products, and culinary experiences.

Galway International Oyster & Seafood Festival
Held annually in Galway City, this iconic festival
celebrates the region's seafood heritage with oyster
shucking competitions, seafood tastings, and live
music. Visitors can sample fresh oysters from local
producers and enjoy a variety of seafood dishes
prepared by top chefs.

Taste of Dublin
Taking place in the heart of Dublin, Taste of Dublin
is a gastronomic extravaganza featuring tastings,
cooking demonstrations, and gourmet experiences
from some of the city's finest restaurants and chefs.
Visitors can indulge in a wide range of culinary
delights, from Irish specialties to international
cuisines, while enjoying live entertainment and
interactive food workshops.

Burren Food Fayre
Held in County Clare, the Burren Food Fayre
celebrates the unique flavors of the Burren region
with a showcase of local artisanal products,
farm-fresh produce, and culinary demonstrations.
Visitors can meet local producers, sample delicious
food and drink, and learn about the sustainable
food practices that make the Burren a culinary
hotspot.

West Waterford Festival of Food
Taking place in Dungarvan, County Waterford, this festival celebrates the best of Irish food and drink with a program of tastings, cookery demonstrations, and food tours. Visitors can explore the picturesque town of Dungarvan and its surrounding countryside while sampling artisanal cheeses, craft beers, and gourmet treats.

- Savour Kilkenny: Held in the medieval city of Kilkenny, Savour Kilkenny is a food festival that celebrates the best of local produce and culinary talent. Visitors can enjoy a packed program of food tastings, cookery demonstrations, and workshops, as well as street food markets and pop-up dining experiences showcasing the flavors of the region.

- Dingle Food Festival: Located on the stunning Dingle Peninsula in County Kerry, this festival celebrates the rich food culture of the region with a program of tastings, demonstrations, and food trails. Visitors can explore the picturesque town of Dingle and its surrounding countryside while sampling fresh seafood, artisanal cheeses, and locally produced meats and vegetables.

These food festivals, among many others held throughout the country, offer a unique opportunity to experience the flavors of Ireland and discover the diverse culinary traditions that make the country a food lover's paradise. Whether you're a seafood aficionado, a cheese connoisseur, or simply looking to indulge in delicious food and drink, Ireland's food festivals are sure to tantalize your taste buds and leave you craving more.

Chapter 7. Accommodation Options

When planning a trip to Ireland, you'll find a wide range of accommodation options to suit every taste, budget, and travel style.

Hotels
Ireland boasts a diverse selection of hotels, ranging from luxurious five-star establishments to charming boutique hotels and budget-friendly options. Whether you're seeking opulent amenities, stunning views, or convenient city-center locations, you'll find a hotel to meet your needs in cities like Dublin, Galway, Cork, and Belfast, as well as in smaller towns and rural areas throughout the country.

Bed and Breakfasts (B&Bs)
For a more personalized and intimate experience, consider staying in a traditional Irish bed and breakfast. Run by friendly local hosts, B&Bs offer comfortable accommodations, home-cooked breakfasts, and insider tips on the best places to explore in the area. Many B&Bs are located in scenic countryside settings, providing a tranquil retreat away from the hustle and bustle of city life.

Guesthouse
Similar to B&Bs, guesthouses in Ireland offer cozy accommodations and warm hospitality in a relaxed atmosphere. With fewer rooms than a hotel, guesthouses provide a more personalized experience and often feature communal areas where guests can socialize and relax. Whether located in a bustling city or a remote village, guesthouses offer a comfortable and welcoming home away from home.

Self-Catering Accommodations
Ideal for families, groups, or travelers seeking greater independence and flexibility, self-catering accommodations such as holiday cottages, apartments, and vacation rentals provide all the comforts of home. With fully equipped kitchens, spacious living areas, and often private gardens or terraces, self-catering accommodations offer the freedom to cook your meals, relax in your own space, and explore the local area at your own pace.

Hostels
Perfect for budget-conscious travelers and backpackers, hostels in Ireland offer affordable accommodations in dormitory-style rooms or

private rooms with shared facilities. With communal kitchens, lounges, and social activities, hostels provide a lively and sociable atmosphere where guests can meet fellow travelers from around the world. Many hostels also offer private rooms and family-friendly accommodations for those seeking a bit more privacy.

Camping and Glamping
For outdoor enthusiasts and nature lovers, camping and glamping (luxury camping) provide an opportunity to immerse yourself in Ireland's stunning landscapes and scenic beauty. From traditional campsites with basic facilities to glamping sites with luxury tents, yurts, and eco-friendly pods, there are plenty of options for camping and glamping throughout the country, including in national parks, coastal areas, and rural retreats.

Unique Accommodations
For a truly unforgettable experience, consider staying in one of Ireland's unique accommodations, such as castles, lighthouses, historic houses, or eco-friendly retreats. These one-of-a-kind properties offer a chance to immerse yourself in

Ireland's rich history, culture, and natural beauty while enjoying modern comforts and amenities.

No matter where you choose to stay during your visit to Ireland, you're sure to find accommodations that suit your preferences and enhance your travel experience. From cozy countryside retreats to elegant city-center hotels, Ireland offers a warm welcome and hospitality that will make you feel right at home.

Hotels and Guesthouses

Ireland, with its stunning landscapes, rich history, and warm hospitality, beckons travelers from around the globe. Whether you're seeking luxury accommodations in bustling cities or quaint guesthouses in tranquil countryside settings, Ireland offers a diverse array of options to suit every traveler's preferences and budget.

Dublin

The Shelbourne, Autograph Collection
Situated in the heart of Dublin, this iconic hotel blends historic charm with contemporary elegance.

With luxurious rooms, award-winning dining, and a prime location near landmarks like Trinity College and St. Stephen's Green, The Shelbourne offers a quintessential Dublin experience.

The Westbury
Nestled in Dublin's vibrant city center, The Westbury captivates guests with its sophisticated ambiance and impeccable service. Indulge in gourmet cuisine at the hotel's renowned restaurants, unwind in stylish accommodations, and explore nearby attractions such as Grafton Street and Dublin Castle.

Ariel House
For a cozy retreat away from the hustle and bustle, Ariel House provides an oasis of tranquility in Dublin's leafy Ballsbridge neighborhood. This charming guesthouse offers elegant rooms, homemade breakfasts, and personalized hospitality, making it a favorite among discerning travelers.

Galway

The Galmont Hotel & Spa
Overlooking Galway Bay, The Galmont Hotel & Spa offers a blend of luxury and relaxation in Ireland's

cultural capital. From spacious rooms with panoramic views to rejuvenating spa treatments and exquisite dining options, this waterfront hotel ensures a memorable stay in Galway.

The House Hotel
Tucked away in Galway's historic Latin Quarter, The House Hotel exudes boutique charm and modern comfort. With stylishly appointed rooms, a cozy cocktail bar, and a central location steps away from Galway's vibrant nightlife and attractions, The House Hotel captures the essence of the city's bohemian spirit.

Cork

The River Lee Hotel
Set along the banks of the River Lee, this contemporary hotel offers a luxurious retreat in Cork's city center. With sleek accommodations, innovative cuisine at The Grill Room, and scenic views of the river and surrounding countryside, The River Lee Hotel provides a memorable urban escape.

Garnish House

For a cozy bed-and-breakfast experience in Cork, Garnish House exudes warmth and hospitality in every detail. Located within walking distance of Cork's historic center, this family-run guesthouse offers comfortable rooms, hearty Irish breakfasts, and personalized recommendations for exploring the city and its attractions.

Killarney

The Europe Hotel & Resort
Set amidst the breathtaking scenery of Killarney National Park, The Europe Hotel & Resort epitomizes luxury and natural beauty. With spacious suites, fine dining overlooking the lakes of Killarney, and world-class spa facilities, this five-star retreat offers an unparalleled Irish getaway.

The Killarney Park Hotel
Nestled in the heart of Killarney town, The Killarney Park Hotel blends traditional elegance with contemporary luxury. From indulgent afternoon teas to sumptuous accommodations and attentive service, this boutique hotel provides a

haven of comfort and sophistication in County Kerry.

From historic landmarks to scenic countryside escapes, Ireland's hotels and guesthouses offer a wealth of experiences for travelers seeking comfort, convenience, and authentic Irish hospitality. Whether you're exploring vibrant cities like Dublin and Galway or venturing into the serene landscapes of Cork and Killarney, these recommended accommodations ensure unforgettable stays in the Emerald Isle.

Bed and Breakfasts

Bed and breakfast accommodations in Ireland epitomize the warmth and hospitality for which the country is renowned. These charming establishments offer guests a cozy and intimate experience, providing a home away from home during their stay.

Warm Hospitality
At the heart of the bed and breakfast experience in Ireland is the genuine warmth and hospitality extended by the hosts. Guests are welcomed with

open arms and treated like family, with hosts often going above and beyond to ensure a memorable stay.

Cozy Accommodation
 B&Bs in Ireland come in a variety of styles, from quaint cottages to elegant townhouses. Each property offers comfortable and tastefully decorated rooms, equipped with all the amenities needed for a relaxing stay, such as plush bedding, en-suite bathrooms, and complimentary toiletries.

Delicious Breakfasts
A highlight of staying at a bed and breakfast in Ireland is the delicious breakfast served each morning. Guests can indulge in a whearty Irish breakfast, featuring traditional favorites like bacon, eggs, sausage, and black pudding, accompanied by freshly brewed coffee and homemade soda bread.

Scenic Locations
Many bed and breakfasts in Ireland boast scenic locations that showcase the country's natural beauty. Guests can wake up to breathtaking views of rolling countryside, tranquil lakes, or rugged coastlines, providing a serene backdrop for their stay.

Personalized Service
Unlike larger hotels, bed and breakfast
accommodations offer personalized service tailored
to the needs and preferences of each guest. Hosts
are often happy to provide recommendations for
local attractions, dining options, and activities,
ensuring that guests make the most of their time in
Ireland.

Value for Money
In addition to offering warm hospitality and cozy
accommodations, bed and breakfasts in Ireland
provide excellent value for money. Rates are
typically more affordable than hotels, making them
an attractive option for travelers seeking an
authentic Irish experience without breaking the
bank.

Overall, bed and breakfast accommodations in
Ireland offer a unique blend of warmth, charm, and
hospitality that embodies the spirit of Irish culture.
Whether traveling for leisure or business, guests
can expect a memorable and enjoyable stay at a
B&B, where they'll be treated to genuine Irish
hospitality and unforgettable experiences.

Hostels and Budget Accommodation

When embarking on an adventure through Ireland, finding suitable accommodation that aligns with your budget is crucial. Fortunately, Ireland offers a diverse range of budget-friendly options, with hostels being a popular choice among travelers seeking affordability, community, and convenience. Let's delve into the world of hostels and other budget accommodations across the Emerald Isle.

Hostels in Ireland cater to a wide range of travelers, from solo backpackers to budget-conscious families. These accommodations typically offer dormitory-style rooms with shared facilities, such as bathrooms and communal kitchens, fostering a social atmosphere where guests can connect and share travel experiences.

Some renowned hostel chains in Ireland include:

Hostelling International (HI)
With numerous locations across the country, HI hostels are known for their quality facilities, friendly staff, and vibrant communal spaces. From

historic buildings to modern accommodations, HI hostels offer something for every traveler.

Barnacles Hostels
Situated in popular destinations like Dublin and Galway, Barnacles Hostels combine affordability with prime locations, making them ideal bases for exploring nearby attractions and nightlife.

Kinlay Hostel Group
Operating in cities like Cork and Galway, Kinlay Hostels provide comfortable lodgings with a focus on guest satisfaction, offering amenities such as free Wi-Fi, organized tours, and on-site bars.

Unique Budget Accommodation Options

Beyond traditional hostels, Ireland boasts several unique budget-friendly accommodations that promise unforgettable experiences:

Farm Stays
Immerse yourself in rural Irish life by staying at a farmstay accommodation. These cozy retreats offer guests the chance to participate in farm activities, savor home-cooked meals, and unwind amidst picturesque countryside scenery.

Guesthouses and B&Bs
While not always considered budget
accommodations, many guesthouses and
bed-and-breakfast establishments in Ireland offer
competitive rates, especially during off-peak
seasons. Enjoy warm hospitality, hearty breakfasts,
and personalized service at these charming
properties.

Campgrounds and Glamping Sites
For nature enthusiasts and adventure seekers,
camping and glamping provide budget-friendly
options for accommodation. Set up your tent under
the stars at a designated campground or indulge in
a more luxurious camping experience with
glamping amenities like comfortable beds, hot
showers, and communal dining areas.

Tips for Booking Budget Accommodation

Plan Ahead
 To secure the best deals and availability, book your
accommodation well in advance, especially during
peak travel seasons like summer and major
holidays.

Consider Off-Peak Travel
Traveling during shoulder seasons or weekdays can result in lower rates and fewer crowds, allowing you to stretch your budget further.

Utilize Booking Platforms
Take advantage of online booking platforms and hostel aggregator websites to compare prices, read reviews, and find exclusive deals on budget accommodations in Ireland.

Stay Flexible
Be open to staying in different types of accommodations, such as mixed dormitories, private rooms, or alternative lodgings like host families or couchsurfing, to find the best value for your budget.

Exploring Ireland on a budget doesn't mean sacrificing comfort or memorable experiences. With an array of hostels, guesthouses, and unique accommodations to choose from, budget travelers can discover the beauty and hospitality of the Emerald Isle without breaking the bank. So pack your bags, set your sights on Ireland, and embark on an affordable adventure filled with culture, history, and unforgettable moments.

110

Chapter 8. Transportation

Getting Around Ireland

Navigating the scenic landscapes and vibrant cities of Ireland is a delightful experience, thanks to the various transportation options available to travelers. Whether you're exploring bustling urban centers or meandering through the countryside, getting around Ireland is convenient, efficient, and often filled with picturesque views.

Public Transportation

Ireland boasts an extensive network of buses, trains, and trams, making public transportation a convenient option for travelers.

Bus Services
Bus Eireann operates a comprehensive bus network connecting major cities, towns, and rural areas across the country. Regional bus services, such as Citylink and GoBus, provide connections between cities like Dublin, Galway, Cork, and Limerick.

Train Services
Irish Rail offers intercity and commuter train services, linking Dublin with key destinations such as Belfast, Galway, Cork, and Waterford. The Dublin Area Rapid Transit (DART) system provides frequent and reliable train services along the scenic coastline of Dublin Bay.

Trams
In Dublin, the Luas tram system serves the city center and surrounding suburbs, offering a convenient way to navigate key attractions and neighborhoods.

Rental Cars

For travelers seeking flexibility and independence, renting a car is an excellent option for exploring Ireland at your own pace.

Car Rental Companies
Major car rental companies like Hertz, Avis, and Europcar have branches at airports and city centers across Ireland, offering a wide selection of vehicles to suit different preferences and budgets.

Driving in Ireland

It's essential to familiarize yourself with Ireland's road rules, including driving on the left-hand side of the road, roundabouts, and speed limits. The country's well-maintained road network provides easy access to scenic routes, historic sites, and charming villages.

Cycling

Exploring Ireland by bicycle offers a unique and immersive way to experience the country's natural beauty and cultural heritage.

Cycling Routes
Ireland features a network of designated cycling routes, including the Wild Atlantic Way, the Great Western Greenway, and the Waterford Greenway, offering cyclists breathtaking scenery and diverse terrain to explore.

Bike Rentals
Many towns and cities in Ireland offer bike rental services, allowing travelers to hire bicycles for short excursions or multi-day adventures. Additionally, accommodations such as guesthouses and hostels

often provide facilities for storing and maintaining bicycles.

Walking

For travelers who prefer a slower pace and closer connection to their surroundings, walking is an ideal way to explore Ireland's cities, towns, and countryside.

Urban Walking Tours
In cities like Dublin, Galway, and Cork, guided walking tours provide insights into local history, culture, and architecture, allowing visitors to discover hidden gems and off-the-beaten-path attractions.

Hiking Trails
Ireland boasts a wealth of hiking trails, ranging from easy coastal walks to challenging mountain treks. Popular routes include the Wicklow Way, the Kerry Way, and the Causeway Coast Way, offering hikers breathtaking views and opportunities to connect with nature.

Getting around Ireland is a seamless and enjoyable experience, thanks to its well-developed transportation infrastructure and diverse travel options. Whether you prefer the convenience of public transportation, the flexibility of renting a car, the freedom of cycling, or the serenity of walking, Ireland offers something for every traveler to explore and discover.

Renting a Car

Renting a car in Ireland offers travelers the freedom to explore the country's diverse landscapes, charming villages, and cultural attractions at their own pace. To begin, it's essential to choose the right rental company. Researching different options allows you to find a company with competitive rates, transparent policies, and a wide selection of vehicles. Popular rental companies in Ireland include Hertz, Avis, Europcar, and Budget, among others.

Booking your rental car well in advance is advisable, especially during peak travel seasons, to ensure availability and secure the best rates. Online booking platforms or direct contact with rental companies can help you compare prices and options. When booking, provide accurate information about your travel dates, pickup/drop-off locations, and any additional equipment or services you may require.

Understanding insurance coverage is crucial when renting a car in Ireland. Most rental car insurance options include Collision Damage Waiver (CDW) and Theft Protection, which reduce your financial liability in case of damage or theft. Consider purchasing additional coverage like Super Collision Damage Waiver (SCDW) or Personal Accident Insurance (PAI) for added peace of mind. Review the terms and conditions of your insurance policy carefully to understand any exclusions, deductibles, or limitations.

Navigating Irish roads requires familiarity with the country's road rules, signage, and driving etiquette. Remember to drive on the left-hand side of the road and exercise caution, especially on narrow, winding roads and in rural areas. GPS navigation systems or mobile apps can be invaluable tools for navigating unfamiliar routes and avoiding getting lost.

When it comes to fueling up, petrol and diesel are the most common fuel options in Ireland, with petrol stations readily available throughout the country. Be sure to fill up your tank before embarking on long journeys, particularly in remote areas where gas stations may be scarce. Pay attention to fuel prices and choose the most cost-effective option for your budget.

Parking in urban areas requires adherence to parking regulations and attention to signage to avoid fines or towing. Utilize designated parking lots or garages whenever possible to ensure the safety of your rental car. In case of emergencies or breakdowns, contact your rental company's roadside assistance service for prompt assistance and support.

When returning your rental car, ensure it's returned on time and in the same condition as when you picked it up to avoid additional fees or penalties. Remove any personal belongings and clean out the vehicle before returning it to the rental company. Allow sufficient time for inspection and paperwork processing upon returning the car to ensure a smooth checkout process.

Renting a car in Ireland offers travelers flexibility, convenience, and the opportunity to create unforgettable memories while exploring the country's scenic beauty and cultural heritage.

Public Transportation

Public transportation in Ireland offers travelers an efficient and convenient way to explore the country's vibrant cities, charming towns, and stunning countryside. With a well-developed network of buses, trains, trams, and ferries, navigating Ireland's diverse landscapes is made accessible to both locals and visitors alike.

Buses serve as the backbone of Ireland's public transportation system, connecting major cities, towns, and rural areas across the country. Operated by both national and regional companies, bus services offer frequent schedules, comfortable seating, and affordable fares. Travelers can easily hop on a bus to explore popular tourist destinations, picturesque villages, and off-the-beaten-path attractions with ease.

For longer journeys and intercity travel, Ireland's extensive railway network provides a reliable and scenic mode of transportation. Irish Rail operates a range of services, including commuter trains, intercity express trains, and scenic routes that traverse the country's breathtaking landscapes. Passengers can sit back, relax, and enjoy panoramic views of rolling hills, coastal cliffs, and picturesque countryside while traveling between destinations.

In urban areas such as Dublin, Cork, and Galway, tram systems offer a convenient way to navigate the bustling city streets. Luas in Dublin and Luas in Cork provide efficient and eco-friendly transportation options for commuters, shoppers, and sightseers, with frequent services running throughout the day and evening. Trams provide easy access to popular attractions, shopping districts, and entertainment venues, reducing reliance on private vehicles and alleviating traffic congestion in city centers.

In addition to buses, trains, and trams, Ireland's public transportation network also includes ferry services that connect the mainland with offshore islands and coastal communities. Ferries operate year-round, offering passengers the opportunity to explore remote islands, rugged coastlines, and scenic harbors dotted along Ireland's coastline.

Whether embarking on a day trip to scenic islands like Inishmore or traveling between coastal towns and cities, ferry services provide a unique and memorable way to experience Ireland's maritime heritage.

To enhance the convenience and accessibility of public transportation, Ireland's transport authorities offer integrated ticketing systems, travel passes, and mobile apps that streamline the journey planning process. Travelers can purchase tickets, plan routes, and access real-time information on schedules and service disruptions, making it easier to navigate Ireland's public transportation network with confidence.

Public transportation in Ireland offers travelers a reliable, affordable, and environmentally friendly way to explore the country's rich cultural heritage, stunning natural landscapes, and vibrant urban centers. Whether embarking on a sightseeing adventure, commuting to work, or simply enjoying a leisurely journey through the Irish countryside, public transportation provides a convenient and enjoyable travel experience for all.

Chapter 9. Practical Information

Emergency Contacts

When traveling to Ireland, it's essential to be prepared for any unexpected situations that may arise. Knowing the appropriate emergency contacts can provide peace of mind and ensure prompt assistance in times of need.

Emergency Services
In case of emergencies requiring immediate medical attention, dialing 999 or 112 will connect you to the Irish emergency services. These numbers are toll-free and can be accessed from any phone, including mobile devices.

Garda Síochána
The national police service of Ireland, Garda Síochána, plays a vital role in maintaining law and order across the country. For non-emergency situations or to report a crime, you can contact your local Garda station. The Garda Confidential Line (1800 666 111) offers a confidential avenue for

reporting information related to criminal activities anonymously.

Ambulance Service
 If you or someone else requires urgent medical assistance, contacting the National Ambulance Service is imperative. Trained paramedics and emergency medical technicians respond to medical emergencies promptly and provide essential pre-hospital care while transporting patients to the nearest medical facility.

Fire Brigade
In the event of a fire or other emergencies requiring the expertise of firefighters, dialing 999 or 112 will connect you to the Fire Brigade. Highly trained firefighters equipped with specialized equipment respond to fire-related incidents, hazardous material spills, and other emergencies to ensure public safety.

Coast Guard
Ireland's Coast Guard provides search and rescue services along the coastline, inland waterways, and mountainous regions. In situations such as maritime distress, water-related accidents, or missing persons cases in coastal areas, contacting

the Coast Guard through 999 or 112 can initiate swift response and rescue operations.

Mountain Rescue
For emergencies occurring in remote or mountainous areas, the Irish Mountain Rescue Service plays a crucial role in providing search and rescue assistance. Trained volunteers equipped with specialized gear and vehicles respond to incidents such as hiking accidents, lost or injured climbers, and medical emergencies in rugged terrain.

Medical Assistance
Beyond emergency services, knowing the contact information for medical facilities and healthcare providers can be beneficial. In non-urgent medical situations, contacting your general practitioner (GP) or visiting a local clinic may be appropriate. Additionally, many pharmacies offer out-of-hours services and can provide advice on minor ailments and medication.

Embassy or Consulate
For travelers requiring assistance with passports, legal issues, or other consular services, contacting your country's embassy or consulate in Ireland is

advisable. Consular officials can provide support and guidance to citizens facing emergencies or difficulties while abroad.

Local Support Services
In addition to emergency services, various local organizations and support groups offer assistance to individuals experiencing crises or seeking help with specific issues. These may include mental health support services, domestic violence shelters, addiction helplines, and community outreach programs.

Being aware of the appropriate emergency contacts in Ireland is essential for ensuring your safety and well-being during your travels. Whether facing medical emergencies, criminal incidents, or natural disasters, knowing how to access emergency services and assistance can make a significant difference in the outcome of any situation. By familiarizing yourself with these contacts and keeping them readily accessible, you can enjoy your time in Ireland with greater peace of mind and confidence in your ability to respond effectively to any unforeseen circumstances.

Health and Safety Tips

Health and safety are paramount considerations for travelers exploring Ireland's captivating landscapes and vibrant cities. Understanding and adhering to best practices ensures a smooth and enjoyable journey while minimizing potential risks.

Health Precautions
Prior to embarking on your Irish adventure, it's advisable to research any necessary vaccinations or health precautions recommended for travelers to the region. While Ireland generally maintains high standards of hygiene and healthcare, it's wise to pack a basic medical kit containing essential items such as over-the-counter medications, adhesive bandages, and antiseptic wipes to address minor ailments or injuries.

Food and Water Safety
Sampling Ireland's renowned culinary delights is a highlight of any visit, but exercising caution when consuming food and beverages is essential. Stick to reputable establishments with high hygiene standards, and opt for bottled water in areas where tap water quality may be uncertain. Additionally, be mindful of potential food allergies or intolerances

when dining out, and communicate your dietary needs clearly to restaurant staff.

Outdoor Safety
Ireland's breathtaking natural landscapes beckon outdoor enthusiasts to explore its rugged coastlines, lush forests, and rolling hills. Whether hiking, cycling, or partaking in water sports, prioritize safety by familiarizing yourself with local terrain and weather conditions, wearing appropriate footwear and protective gear, and adhering to designated trails and safety guidelines. It's also wise to carry a map, compass, or GPS device when venturing into remote areas.

Road Safety
Navigating Ireland's scenic roadways offers an excellent way to experience the country's picturesque scenery and charming villages. However, it's essential to exercise caution and familiarity with local traffic laws and regulations. Drive on the left side of the road, adhere to speed limits, and remain vigilant for narrow roads, sharp turns, and livestock crossings, particularly in rural areas. Additionally, ensure your vehicle is properly maintained and equipped with safety essentials such as seatbelts and reflective vests.

Weather Awareness
Ireland's climate is characterized by its variability, with rain showers and gusty winds common throughout the year. Stay informed about weather forecasts and prepare accordingly by packing waterproof clothing, sturdy footwear, and layers to adjust to changing conditions. In the event of severe weather warnings, exercise caution and consider postponing outdoor activities until conditions improve to ensure your safety.

Emergency Preparedness
Familiarize yourself with emergency contact information, including local emergency services, medical facilities, and embassy or consulate details for your country of residence. Carry a fully charged mobile phone with you at all times and share your travel itinerary with trusted individuals. In the event of an emergency, remain calm, assess the situation, and seek assistance promptly from local authorities or emergency services.

Cultural Sensitivity
Respect for local customs, traditions, and etiquette is integral to fostering positive interactions and minimizing cultural misunderstandings.

Familiarize yourself with Irish customs, greetings, and social norms, and approach interactions with openness, curiosity, and courtesy. Remember to ask for permission before photographing individuals or sensitive sites, and refrain from engaging in behaviors that may be perceived as disrespectful or intrusive.

Priority health and safety considerations enhances the overall travel experience in Ireland, allowing visitors to immerse themselves fully in the country's rich culture, natural beauty, and warm hospitality. By adopting a proactive approach to health precautions, outdoor safety, road awareness, weather preparedness, and cultural sensitivity, travelers can enjoy a memorable and fulfilling journey while minimizing potential risks and hazards.

Communication and Internet Access

Communication and internet access in Ireland are integral aspects of modern travel and daily life. As a technologically advanced country, Ireland offers a robust communication infrastructure that ensures seamless connectivity for both residents and visitors alike.

In terms of mobile communication, Ireland boasts several major network providers, including Vodafone, Three, Eir, and Tesco Mobile, offering extensive coverage across the country. These providers offer various prepaid and postpaid plans catering to different usage needs and budgets. Visitors can easily purchase prepaid SIM cards at airports, convenience stores, and mobile phone shops, allowing them to stay connected during their stay in Ireland.

Additionally, Ireland's public Wi-Fi infrastructure is well-developed, with many hotels, restaurants, cafes, and public spaces offering free Wi-Fi access to patrons. This widespread availability of Wi-Fi makes it convenient for travelers to stay connected while exploring cities or relaxing in local establishments. However, it's advisable to exercise caution when using public Wi-Fi networks, as they may not always be secure, and sensitive information could be at risk of interception.

For those who require constant internet access, renting a portable Wi-Fi hotspot or pocket Wi-Fi device is a viable option. Several companies in Ireland provide rental services for these devices, allowing travelers to enjoy reliable internet connectivity wherever they go, without relying on public Wi-Fi networks or incurring high roaming charges.

Furthermore, Ireland's telecommunications infrastructure supports various communication channels, including voice calls, text messaging, and internet-based communication platforms such as WhatsApp, Skype, and Zoom. These platforms enable individuals to stay in touch with friends, family, and colleagues, whether they're traveling within Ireland or communicating with contacts overseas.

In terms of internet access at accommodations, most hotels, hostels, and guesthouses in Ireland provide complimentary Wi-Fi for guests. This amenity ensures that travelers can stay connected and access essential online services, such as email, social media, and travel apps, from the comfort of their accommodation.

Moreover, Ireland's urban centers are equipped with modern telecommunications infrastructure, including high-speed broadband networks, ensuring fast and reliable internet access for residents and businesses. This connectivity facilitates remote work, online education, and digital innovation, contributing to Ireland's position as a tech-savvy nation.

In conclusion, communication and internet access in Ireland are readily available and accessible, enhancing the overall travel experience for visitors. Whether through mobile networks, public Wi-Fi, portable Wi-Fi devices, or traditional communication channels, travelers can stay connected and informed while exploring the Emerald Isle. With a strong emphasis on connectivity and technological innovation, Ireland continues to be a welcoming destination for both leisure and business travelers seeking seamless communication solutions.

Money-Saving Tips

When planning a trip to Ireland, managing your budget wisely can enhance your travel experience and allow you to make the most of your adventure on the Emerald Isle. Here are some practical tips to help you save money while exploring Ireland.

Flexible Travel Dates and Accommodation Choices
Flexibility with your travel dates and accommodation choices can significantly impact your overall expenses. Consider traveling during off-peak seasons or weekdays when prices for flights, accommodations, and attractions are often lower. Additionally, exploring alternative lodging options such as hostels, guesthouses, or vacation rentals can provide significant savings compared to traditional hotels.

Public Transportation and Carpooling
Opting for public transportation, such as buses and trains, instead of renting a car can help reduce transportation costs while allowing you to experience the scenic beauty of Ireland's countryside. Many cities and towns in Ireland are well-connected by reliable and affordable public transit networks. Additionally, carpooling or ridesharing services can be economical alternatives for short-distance travel or exploring remote areas.

Budget-Friendly Dining Options

Sampling Ireland's culinary delights doesn't have to break the bank. Look for local pubs, cafes, and markets that offer affordable meals and traditional Irish dishes. Take advantage of early bird specials, lunch deals, or prix fixe menus offered by restaurants to enjoy delicious meals at discounted prices. Additionally, consider self-catering by purchasing groceries from supermarkets and preparing your meals, especially for breakfast and lunch, to save on dining expenses.

Discounts and Free Attractions
Take advantage of discounts, coupons, and special offers available for attractions, tours, and activities in Ireland. Many museums, galleries, and historical sites offer reduced admission fees for students, seniors, or groups. Research free or low-cost attractions, such as public parks, scenic walks, and cultural events, that allow you to explore Ireland's natural beauty and cultural heritage without spending a fortune.

Avoid Tourist Traps
Be mindful of tourist traps and overpriced tourist areas where prices for goods and services are inflated. Instead, seek out authentic experiences and local establishments frequented by residents,

where prices are often more reasonable and reflective of the true value. Engage with locals, explore hidden gems, and immerse yourself in the local culture to discover genuine Irish hospitality and save money in the process.

Pack Wisely and Plan Ahead
Packing essentials such as reusable water bottles, snacks, and rain gear can help you save money on incidental expenses while traveling in Ireland. Plan your itinerary in advance, research transportation options, and book accommodations, activities, and tours ahead of time to take advantage of early booking discounts and avoid last-minute price surges.

By implementing these money-saving tips and adopting a mindful approach to budgeting and spending, you can enjoy an unforgettable travel experience in Ireland without overspending. Embrace the charm, hospitality, and natural beauty of the Emerald Isle while keeping your finances in check, allowing you to create lasting memories without financial stress.

Chapter 10. Language Guide

Common Phrases in Irish

Ireland, with its rich Gaelic heritage, boasts a unique language that reflects its cultural identity. Whether you're planning a trip to the Emerald Isle or simply curious about the Irish language, familiarizing yourself with some common phrases can enhance your experience and appreciation of Irish culture. Here are some essential phrases to get you started:

Greetings and Basic Phrases

Dia duit (dee-ah gwitch) - Hello (literally "God be with you")
Conas atá tú? (kun-us ah-taw too) - How are you?
Go raibh maith agat (guh rev mah ah-gut) - Thank you
Slán (slawn) - Goodbye
Cén t-am é? (kayn tahm ay) - What time is it?

Introductions and Polite Expressions

Is mise... (iss mish-eh) - I am...

Tá mé ag foghlaim Gaeilge (taw may egg foh-lim
gayl-ga) - I am learning Irish
Tá brón orm (taw bron or-um) - I'm sorry
Le do thoil (leh duh hull) - Please
Go raibh míle maith agat (guh rev meela mah
ah-gut) - Thank you very much

Common Phrases for Everyday Situations

An bhfuil an leithreas anseo? (ahn will un leh-hras
ahn-shuh) - Is the restroom here?
Cá bhfuil an stáisiún traenach? (kah will un
staw-shoon traw-nukh) - Where is the train station?
An bhfuil tú in ann cuidiú liom? (ahn will too in ahn
kwi-doo lum) - Can you help me?
Céard é sin? (kayrd ay shin) - What is that?
An bhfuil cead agam dul go dtí an leithreas? (ahn
will cadd ah-gum dull guh dee un leh-hras) - May I
go to the restroom?

Expressions for Food and Drink

Ólann mé tae (awl-awn may tay) - I drink tea
Bíonn sé ag cur báistí go minic (bee-un shay egg kur
bawsh-tee guh min-ik) - It often rains
Is maith liom cáca milis (iss mah lum kaw-kah
mill-ish) - I like cake

An bhfuil rud ar bith níos saoire? (ahn will rud air bith nee-iss seer-uh) - Is there anything cheaper?
Ba mhaith liom stobhach (bah why lum stuh-vukh) - I would like porridge

Travel and Directions

Céard atá ar siúl? (kayrd ah-taw air shool) - What's happening?
An bhfuil an traein go hAill na nGall? (ahn will un trane guh hill nah ngawl) - Is the train to Donegal?
Cén áit í? (kayn awt ee) - Where is it?
An bhfuil aon thaispeántas ann? (ahn will ayn hays-pwant-iss ahn - Is there an exhibition there?
Cén áit atá tú ag iarraidh dul? (kayn awt ah-taw too egg eer-ee gull) - Where do you want to go?

Learning and using these common Irish phrases can enrich your interactions with locals and deepen your understanding of Irish culture. Whether you're ordering food in a traditional pub, asking for directions, or simply exchanging pleasantries, incorporating a few phrases in Irish can make your experience in Ireland even more memorable.

Made in the USA
Las Vegas, NV
17 November 2024

11979738R30079